The Grief Trip

The Grief Trip

Learning To Heal WITH Grief

and Psychedelics

Stuart Preston

David,

Thank you so much for the opportunity to speak to your Death & Dying class. And thank you for the important work you do!

Stuart

Acknowledgements

A big thank you to my wife and editor, Cynthia, for the support, encouragement, and editing of this book, including making sure the memories I included here are correct. And there's no way I would have been able to heal with my grief without the love and support from both her and my daughter.

Thank you to Domonic Patrick for the amazing cover art. Dom has been with me making me look good with his design genius through many businesses, The Stoned Ape Show, and now this book.

I'm grateful to everyone along my path who helped me, from teachers to facilitators/shamans, to online communities, local groups, counselors, treasured friends, and family. So many of you have listened to me with open hearts, attended my talks, and supported my work. I can't thank you enough.

And finally, I'm grateful for psychedelics.

The Grief Trip

Introduction

I'm learning to heal with my grief, not from it, with the help of psychedelics.

Let me start this off with a couple of caveats. I'm not recommending that you do drugs to cope with your grief. I'm not recommending drugs, period. Not even psychedelics - entheogens - plant medicines - whatever we call them. They are not for everybody. In fact, I might even say they're not for many. There are some people who should NOT take them.

I do think psychedelics can help get you to where you want to be -- into a place of love, healing, and an understanding of the mechanics of suffering. Psychedelics can help open doors and prepare you for each new message you need to hear as you heal with your grief. They'll help your story unfold, chapter by chapter. Those are both concepts, by the way, from the man I consider to be my teacher, Ram Dass. But there are many paths to those lessons. You don't need psychedelics or Ram Dass to get there. The key is to find your own path. Mine started with mushrooms.

If psychedelics are for you, they'll let you know. They'll find you, so to speak. I'm not a mystical person -- not "woo-woo" as they say. Okay, maybe a little. Because I do believe that when you're ready, psychedelics will be there for you.

Second caveat: they're also illegal. They are still (as of this writing, fingers crossed that it changes soon) Schedule 1 narcotics with the Drug Enforcement Administration (DEA), making it a federal crime to possess, purchase, sell, ship, etc. In most states and local municipalities, they are also still illegal. So, find a legal way to access these (there are a few mentioned in the appendices). Many regions are working on decriminalization. If you can't do that and need to go underground, be safe and discreet, and have good intentions. The point is to heal with your grief.

If you have experienced a deep loss and suffer from grief, there is hope. I don't know that the sadness will ever go away. It hasn't for me. But there can be happiness and joy in life. Since losing my son, Ian, I have sunk low in grief, felt helpless and hopeless. But I have also experienced some pretty remarkable changes, including a strengthened relationship with my wife, a reconnection to my mother, and a growing relationship with my daughter. I've lost 60+ pounds, mostly stopped drinking, started eating better, have a more consistent exercise program, and awakened my 'spiritual' self (this is really the center of it all). That has all helped me create The Stoned Ape Show and podcast as well as offer Sound meditations. I spend more time meditating and feel more compassionate and connected to other humans. I am less judgmental. And my community has grown, with some really incredible people. Those are the changes that came to me. The message of this book is not some self-help success guide. It's not: "You can have it all in the face of your grief. Just get over it!" No. The message is more: "Here's one way of many that you can heal and maybe find some joy in life, all while fully experiencing your grief."

How is that possible? Drugs. More specifically, psychedelics. Some call them medicines, some call them entheogens. I just call them what they are: psychedelics. You see, soon after we lost Ian, my lifetime drug-free self saw an article about how LSD and magic mushrooms can put one into a dreamlike state. I thought, "Well, I already have pretty realistic dreams. Maybe I can dream with Ian." To have him in my dreams would be wonderful, so I decided to try drugs. I started with magic mushrooms.

I ended up going down Alice's rabbit hole, and my whole life changed. Know that, regardless of the "magic" in "magic mushrooms", these substances are not a magic cure for grief and sadness. They simply open up a door and allow you to receive important messages, lessons that are already in your head, that you simply need to uncover. But they can be profound life changing lessons and epiphanies.

As a result of my grief trip with psychedelics, I have discovered a key to finding moments of happiness in life, which has allowed me to get real with my grief and my love for my son, Ian, and my love for everyone. I almost described this trip as finding the "secret" to being happy, but it's no secret. I'm not going to try and teach you the way, because you have your own path, your own way -- which is the point. Once you find your path and get centered on it, you'll be able to work with your grief, find happiness, and learn to heal WITH your grief.

One last point before I dive into this: it's okay to be happy. It takes nothing away from your love for your lost loved one. Nothing. In fact, it may help you develop that love. It can help you find real moments to be with them, in the moment, right here and now.

And finally, before we get on with this, I want you to know that I love you, too. I'm so sorry for your loss. Grief is a motherfucker, and I'm happy that you're looking for a way to heal with your grief. I'm with you, my brother/sister.

And man, do I miss my son.

Part 1: The Loss

"Hey kiddo, you around?"

That was about four o'clock on a Wednesday, two days before Ian and I would celebrate our shared birthday. Ian hadn't shown up to work that day, and his boss called me asking if I'd seen or heard from him. I hadn't, but I didn't normally hear from him during the day.

Ian was a hard worker. He was often the first guy to work, opening up the collaborative workspace where he worked. When his boss told me Ian hadn't shown up, I told him I thought that was unusual for Ian. He said, "I know. Ian is the most punctual employee I've ever had!" We were both worried.

Ian was nineteen years old. He had started his career as a software engineer at fifteen and moved out of the house at seventeen. I had to sign for his auto loan, his apartment, insurance, etc. But he was good for it all. Heck, he made more money than I did! But now he was just nineteen. A kid, in my eyes. So, I still worried about him. The irony is that I stopped worrying about his mental health. He'd gone to a doctor and gotten some medication as an adult, and he really seemed to be doing well -- not that I ever had any kind of serious concern. It's just that finally, I was confident that this young man was well equipped to head out into the world and find his place.

So, I got into my car and started the half-hour drive to Ian's apartment in downtown Phoenix. On the way, I called my wife, to catch her up and let her know that everything was going to be okay and that I'd call when I had more info. Then, I called Ian's apartment complex.

See, Ian had Type 1 diabetes. That's the kind of diabetes that requires insulin injections a few times a day. There are two types of insulin. One he took with meals. The other he injected at night before bed. If he messed up and took the meal insulin at bedtime, it could crash his blood sugar and have serious effects - even coma and death. So, I was worried that this might be what happened. He had made this mistake a few times when he still lived at home, but we were there to help. I called the apartment complex to let them know I hadn't heard from him today, and that I was on my way. They told me a couple of friends of his had shown up to look for him, and that the police were on their way to do a welfare check.

After those calls, I still had a good twenty-plus minutes to go until I got there. I started going over all of the possibilities. Maybe he's been hit by a car or truck while riding his bike around town. He had a tendency to pedal through danger just because he had the right of way. Maybe he had been attacked by a dog while running -- something he'd told me about before. My mind was racing. But you know as a parent, how you can tell, you just know that your kid is alright? Well, I wasn't getting that feeling.

When I pulled up to his apartment complex, there was an official-looking police van parked at the round-about leading into his parking garage. I drove by it and looped my way up to the top floor of the structure, where Ian's apartment was -- the third floor.

When I got there, I noticed the police. There were a couple of police cars and plenty of emergency and official-looking people milling around. But nobody was in a hurry. They weren't behaving as if there was a life to be saved. Denial set in, but it didn't stay long.

"Are you Ian's father?", the officer asked me as I walked up towards Ian's apartment.

"Yes."

"Mr. Preston, I'm sorry to tell you that your son has died...It was a suicide." A suicide. I was expecting to hear that my beloved son had died, but I was dropped into another realm by that word. "Suicide". The office told me that the social workers, the trauma response team, would be talking with me later. He pointed out the two guys who were the friends the apartment had told me about. Then he told me it would be a little bit until they processed my son's body and brought him out.

I went and sat in my car. I could see the scene behind me in my rearview mirror. I look at Ian's friends. "One of them must've given him the gun. Ian was too young to buy one." That's what I thought. I started to blame them. I needed somebody to blame. That blame turned into anger.

I had to make a call, an unimaginable call. I had to tell my wife that her baby, her first-born, was gone. The sound that she made when she heard the news wasn't even human. Later, I learned that she tried to shield herself from our daughter so that she wouldn't traumatize her -- just in case the news was bad. "Ian's gone," is what I said to her. You're not supposed to say that, as it's vague. "Gone? Like out to dinner?" And that's just what she thought, "He's not there? He's out there somewhere, maybe hurt?" But she was afraid of where I was going next. No, Ian was dead, by suicide. Her life changed forever right at that moment.

"We're going to be okay. We're going to make it through this, as a family." It was all I knew to say, to be strong, and provide some foundation, some hope. Hope. What a joke. But that's what I said. We stayed connected, in sobbing silence, for a few more seconds (hours, it felt like). My next call was to my mother.

"Ian died. It was a suicide. Can you call the rest of the family?" I had no right to dump that news on my mom and then give her a job to do. But that's what I did, and she did it. And I'll always be grateful to her for taking that on.

Then, I just sat in my car, in total abject shock. It felt like my heart stopped beating but the air around me took over and was squeezing me like a reverse heartbeat. I just sat in my car, staring at nothing. People ask me when the moment came that I knew that my life had changed forever. I knew before the air left that police officer's vocal cords. "...died...suicide..." I knew right then that nothing could ever be the same again.

I watched my son's covered body emerge from his apartment, wheeled out on a gurney. The emergency professionals -- I don't know if they were cops or medical people as reality had not yet returned -- told me where I could put my hands to feel my boy's body underneath the plastic. I put one hand behind his head, the other on his chest where his hands were crossed and placed my head on his chest. I said goodbye, and he was wheeled off into the back of a truck. He was gone.

The sun was setting, and only a few people remained in the parking lot. As Ian's body got packed away, I got into my car and made the infinite drive home.

That night when I finally crawled into bed, I was afraid to go to sleep. I worried that I'd wake up in the morning having forgotten that Ian was gone and have to relive the loss all over again. I spent the whole night in a half-sleep, pondering this new life.

My grief had just begun.

The Days that Followed

A bomb went off, and my ears didn't stop ringing for weeks. I made my way through those days on autopilot, disoriented, with my mind suspended in confusion. Family started arriving to help, and we had a ceremony to plan.

We had more than a ceremony to plan. As I mentioned, Ian died two days before our shared birthday, which also happened to be five days after his mother's birthday, nine days before Christmas, and ten days before his sister's birthday. Yes, it was a tough time to lose our son and brother.

The last time we saw Ian was celebrating my wife's birthday with a Korean dinner followed by a walk through our local bird sanctuary. Ian seemed to be in a good mood, making hilarious jokes about the holiday lights at the park and being his normal sardonic self. The hoodie he wore that night still sits slung over "his" chair at our dining room table.

When I tell people about the timing of his death -- the birthdays and the holidays -- it makes them just drop in sadness. But I always tell them that losing a child is so unbelievably awful, that it really isn't, can't be, worse just because of the timing. And that's true. Each year, when we get to that time of year, the sadness starts to swell in our hearts, but it's not necessarily compounded by the time of year for me.

I remember, though, getting a Christmas tree soon after he died, after that dark night. I was coming home from the funeral home that handled the cremation and realized that we needed a Christmas tree. One part of my heart was heavy with grief and another part wanted a "normal" life for my daughter. I had no idea that wasn't possible for her to have, not possible for any of us, but I thought it was my duty to try. So I stopped in at Lowe's to find a tree. By this time, so close to the holiday, all the natural trees were gone and the tree lot was cleaned up. I went inside to see what they had in artificial trees. One. They had one tree. I don't mean one kind of tree. I mean one, single tree. It was $160. I carried the boxed tree to my car, struggling to hold myself together.

My mom had spread the word of Ian's death to my side of the family, but I still found myself having to tell my friends, co-workers, and other people in my and Ian's network. I'll never forget his first boss, the man who gave Ian a start on his software engineering path, calling me when he heard, in disbelief and tears, standing outside a movie theater with his family. His life had just changed forever, too. That was a common reaction.

I reached out to a local tech blog -- also owned by that first boss -- to let them know. The writer called me back and interviewed me about Ian, the latest news, and so on. I was very honest with her about the cause of death. At the end of the interview, she asked me, "So, can I include the cause of death in the article?" I didn't know better, or worse, than to say, "Yes, of course. That's the truth." Since then, I've come to notice news of a young person's death indicating that the family wants privacy or some other non-info on how their beloved child had died. Families don't like to talk about suicideor drug overdose -- same thing, really. They are sad and in shock and don't realize they're making things worse by keeping it a secret. They keep the stigma of suicide going, which keeps those suffering quiet and in danger.

———————

Planning a funeral for your own kid is surreal. Funerals are so morbid. The alternative is a "life celebration," something that just doesn't seem fitting for a nineteen-year-old, for a young man who'd chosen to take his own life. But that's what we did.

We rented out a church for a couple of hours. It was a Universalist Unitarian church, a church we had attended a few times as a family, the four of us. We're not religious, and the ceremony was complete without mention of any religion. It was a place we could book on short notice and afford.

We hired a compassionate officiant to run the ceremony. The ceremony was a short opening followed by the eulogy, followed by friends and family coming to the front to share their memories of Ian. Ears still ringing from the shock, I set down to write Ian's eulogy[1].

The ceremony was tough, but it went smoothly. I had prepared myself to avoid breaking down into sobs by doing short, staccato breaths whenever I started to lose it. I made it through the eulogy, driven by my love and admiration for Ian. When I was finished, many others got up and shared their memories and thoughts of Ian, including his mother's proud and sorrowful words. It was beautiful and important.

Our extended family was amazing, helping with every aspect of setting up and tearing down the ceremony.

In my mind, we marked the end of the ear-ringing, dazed phase of our loss when we built Ian's shrine in his bedroom. Doing that actually took us a few months spurred by our daughter's persistence and encouragement as we found accomplishing anything difficult. I think, deep down, we didn't want to do it, as if it made things real and final.

We bought a little bureau online. I built it, and we set on it some reminders of kiddo: his watch, his urn, awards, his GED, and his vanity license plate -- "GED LOL". I visit the shrine each night before I go to bed. It is

---

[1]

http://www.ianprestonmemorialfund.org/ian-preston--memories--complete-badass

the last physical connection to Ian, a place I can go to be with him.

But our family's grief lived well outside the walls of his bedroom.

Our Family in Grief

When I share my story of loss with other people, they often respond with, "I can't even imagine what you're going through." And they're right. Nothing in life is ever as bad as we expect, from dental work to delivering bad news -- except for this grief. It is so much worse than any of us can imagine. The sadness goes deep, deep down into the soul. I described it as being like having an iron vice gripping my heart. My heart felt like it could never relax and provide a full, healthy heartbeat. It is a core sadness.

In those first days, weeks, and months, the grief doesn't recede. It's always there. But it takes on different patterns. I describe it like the chart below. The intensity of the grief never reduces, but the frequency and duration spread out a little bit. In those early days, I may have gone a week or two without having a grief peak, and that peak may have only lasted a couple of days instead of weeks. Even later on, as I write this, those peaks might even be less than a day or just a few minutes. I might still break into tears in the middle of a run.

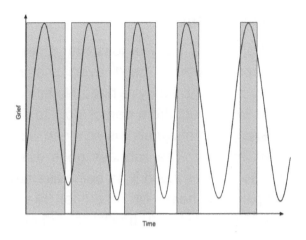

My wife and I also tag-teamed the grief in those early days. It's like we knew subconsciously when the other was hurting so that we could be strong and present for the other and for our daughter. It's a system of symbiotic, complementary grief. I could almost predict when she was down because I was having an "up" period. This grief is so deep and strong, that for both of us to sink down could have been catastrophic for the family. Throughout all of this, I worried that my daughter stayed strong for us, like I was trying to do (for them).

Having an "up" period could be destroyed in an instant by what we call a landmine. Landmines came in all forms. Sometimes it was a young man with Ian's build walking down the street, or a kid wearing a snapback hat, or hearing a Megadeth or Slayer song, or an aroma, or a memory. There were and continue to be so many landmines. When we stepped on one of these, just like a deadly explosive, grief filled our hearts like a fire of sadness, dropping us into an instant depression.

Is grief the same as being depressed? I don't want to diminish what those who suffer from real depression experience, but I get a taste of that blackness on the worst days. On those days, I can't work. I don't want to talk to any other humans -- I mean, even less than normal. All I wanted to do was go eat lunch with my wife or sit with my daughter and have a moment of shared grief and understanding.

The last piece to our family's puzzle of grief is how our friends and family handled our loss and our grief. There are basically three reactions: those who continue to check in on us, those who remain in our lives but don't mention our loss, and those who just flat out disappear.

I don't blame people who disappear. I mean, what do you say to somebody who lost a child? Okay, I'll answer that. You simply say, at first, "I'm sorry to hear about your loss." That's it. You can deliver some food. That'd be appreciated, but you don't need to feel like there's something you need to do. If there is something you can do, that'll come up for you, and you'll offer. Don't put pressure on yourself.

But it seems as though that some people can't get themselves to that point, and they say nothing. And that nothing compounds to the point that they disappear.

Then, there are the friends and family who do stick around. Some do well in checking to make sure we're okay, some don't. Here's the thing. It feels nice when people acknowledge our loss. Don't worry about causing us pain. We're already in pain. The chance of you making it worse is pretty slim. So, if you know somebody who has lost a child, ask them how they're doing. Bring up their child's name, share memories. They will cherish that.

It's better to say something stupid than to stay silent, but there are things that sting. In fact, I came close to punching out a fellow comedian who said this to me: "Suicide is the coward's way out." Wow. He came pretty close to dying that night. I still don't answer his calls. That was bad. But other things are just not great things to say, either, including:

- "He's in a better place."
- "At least you have your daughter."
- "Everything happens for a reason."
- "God has a plan" or "Now, he's with God."

Just avoid those or any version of those, and go with, "I'm sorry for your loss." And you can add, "My heart is with you" for good measure.

Traditional Grief Healing

I like to joke that when Ian died, friends and family kept telling me to go to therapy -- and they did, over and over again. And I thought, "I'm sure that's a great idea...but I'm going to try magic mushrooms!" Which I did. But my wife and I also tried a couple of grief groups. I'm not going to recommend one path as the way to go, but I think it's important to lay down an understanding of what grief is. That way, in the context of your path and the path of psychedelics, you can understand what may be going on.

What Is Grief?

The Mayo Clinic puts it well: "Grief is the natural reaction to loss." It is a broken heart, sometimes literally (see takotsubo cardiomyopathy[2], a heart condition brought on by deep emotion, including grief). This natural reaction needs to play out and cannot be controlled, regardless of how often people in your life tell you, or imply, that you need to get over it. A therapist of mine puts it well, "It's about moving forward, not moving on." You get it. There is no moving on or getting over your loss. So, don't try.

Symptoms of Grief

There are symptoms of grief, and there are stages of grief. The famous five stages of grief (Elisabeth

---

[2]

https://www.health.harvard.edu/heart-health/takotsubo-cardiomyopathy-broken-heart-syndrome

Kübler-Ross's five stages: denial, anger, bargaining, depression, and acceptance) were developed around those suffering from an illness, a potentially terminal illness. Those stages have been applied to those in grief from loss and that has been discounted lately. A friend of mine, Dr. Oren Cox, is a grief therapist, and he holds that there is still value in understanding those stages. Dr. Cox says, "Denial, anger, bargaining, depression, and acceptance -- we know that they are not the sole thing, by any means, but they are the foundation that helped us build all the other frameworks [around grief therapy] and it shouldn't be dismissed". Take that for what you will. Does it apply to you?

For me, I fought against denial. I was afraid of denial. I felt that if I denied Ian's death that I'd have to live it over and over again. I was sure I could not survive that. So, I worked to keep the loss at the top of my mind. That first night without him, I was so afraid I'd sleep and dream and wake up thinking the whole thing was a nightmare. As a result, I kept myself on the edge of sleep that night.

As for the other stages, I just don't feel them. Anger? I wanted to be angry. At the time, I was a very vengeful person. One of my favorite movies was Unforgiven, and I could watch that revenge scene over and over (Crackling thunder, then "Who's the fella owns this shithole?" Boom!). But there was nobody to be angry at, other than myself. Bargaining? Too late for that. Acceptance? This kind of loss is so sudden, real, and permanent, that it's nearly impossible to deny, which drops harsh acceptance right on my lap. Depression? Yeah.

I'll get into more details of sadness and depression later on. Let's just say that sadness comes on by its own will and can gather enough energy to drop me into a depression. You know the feeling.

There are a zillion symptoms of grief, including some of these (per WebMD[3]):

- Nausea
- Shortness of breath (call your doctor!)
- Dry mouth
- Reduced appetite
- Fatigue

There's also complicated grief (Mayo[4]) which will feel a lot more like depression. Just know that your feelings are yours, they're complicated, and they can really suck at times.

I'll circle back to grief again later.

Okay, enough of that. You came for the drugs. Let's do drugs now.

---

[3]

https://www.webmd.com/special-reports/grief-stages/20190711/how-grief-affects-your-body-and-mind
[4]

https://www.mayoclinic.org/diseases-conditions/complicated-grief/symptoms-causes/syc-20360374

Part 2: The Rabbit Hole

Finding the Medicine

The night Ian died, I decided to be strong for my family. Right there, that night, sitting in my car in his parking garage lot, I called my wife and told her we'd survive. I put on my armor and prepared to be the stable rock my family needed. I didn't know that what I was actually doing was hiding until I saw a scene in the movie *What Dreams May Come* with Robin Williams and Annabella Sciorra. They played two parents who had lost their kids in a car wreck, and Robin's father character tried to be strong but ended up not being present for his own healing, stuffing it all inside instead. My wife will attest to the fact that I didn't completely hide, but I think I was taking on a bit in that "strong dad" role.

Then, I read this article about LSD and Magic Mushrooms and how they could drop one into a dream-like state. I thought, well, I have pretty vivid dreams. Maybe with the help of these substances, I can have a realistic dream with Ian in it. It's not the real thing, but it could be better than nothing. So, I started doing some research.

A Quick History Of Psychedelics

There are tons of really good books that cover the history of psychedelics in great detail. Here's the list I have on my website[5]:

- *The Psychedelic Explorer's Guide* by James Fadiman. This is THE resource for understanding your journey, how to experience it, and how to integrate it.
- *The Harvard Psychedelic Club: How Timothy Leary, Ram Dass, Huston Smith, and Andrew Weil Killed the Fifties and Ushered in a New Age for America* I picked this one up during my stay at The Peyote Way Church. It's a great overview of how these pioneers lost control in the 60s/70s, with good biographical info on these pioneers.
- *Be Here Now* by Ram Dass. This book isn't specifically about psychedelics, but I'd be personally remiss if I didn't include it. LSD and mushrooms were central to Richard Alpert's journey to becoming Ram Dass. And the book does mention the importance of accessing new realities and non-ordinary states of consciousness. If you enjoy that, I'd also recommend his autobiography, *Being Ram Dass*
- *How To Change Your Mind* by Michael Pollan. I didn't love this book (or his live talk about it), but everybody else does. He writes about his

---

[5] https://stonedapecomedy.com/psychedelic-resources/

experiences with psychedelics and includes background information.

- *Your Psilocybin Mushroom Companion* by Michelle Janikian. My first journey was with mushrooms. If you're thinking that way, get this book. It's a perfect resource for the teachers. Michelle was also on my podcast, The Stoned Ape Reports.

- Dr. Ben Sessa[6] has a great paper on this: *From Sacred Plants to Psychotherapy: The History and Re-Emergence of Psychedelics in Medicine*

Psychedelic studies in psychology gained real traction starting in the early 1900s, and continued to expand more quickly with the invention of LSD by Albert Hoffman with the Sandoz Pharmaceutical Company in Switzerland. His first "trip" with LSD is still celebrated among us psychonauts/intranauts as "Bicycle Day", referencing his famous LSD-laden bicycle ride home from work that day.

The Grateful Dead and their circle of "deadheads", concurrently with that group at Harvard (Leary & Alpert), started handing out LSD and psilocybin, turning people on and fueling the hippie generation. Richard Nixon wanted to throw African Americans in jail and quiet the

---

6

https://www.rcpsych.ac.uk/docs/default-source/members/sigs/spirituality-spsig/ben-sessa-from-sacred-plants-to-psychotherapy.pdf anti-war hippies, so he made drugs illegal, and created the scheduling of drugs. Psychedelics became Schedule 1 drugs -- deemed harmful and addictive -- and essentially got shut down.

Today, we're experiencing a renaissance, a third wave, of psychedelic use. Churches and Ayahuasca centers are opening up, like the Peyote Way Church, the Church of the Eagle and the Condor, Soul Quest. Studies and funding for studies are growing all over the globe. Societies everywhere are starting to see the benefit of psychedelics and psychedelic therapy.

During my own therapy session, I mentioned my plant medicine use to my therapist. She immediately asked, "Are you high right now?" I can't blame her for that question. We had a short discussion, and I shared the link to my Stoned Ape Show[7]. She came back to me and asked, "If psychedelics are so powerful, why are you talking to me?" Because there's something to be said for combining good therapy with the insight gained from psychedelic journeys. And now, she's on her way to getting certified by MAPS as a psychedelic therapist.

Throw Aldous Huxley and Ken Kesey into the mix, and you have quite a colorful history of psychedelics in America.

---

[7]

https://www.youtube.com/watch?v=GXXxfzvQTW0&feature=yout u.be (Link may not be available)

I'd be remiss if I didn't mention Maria Sabina. Her story is seminal to magic mushrooms in America. It's also a tragic story. She was a curandera - a shaman who worked with the mushrooms in ceremonies called veladas. One day, Gordon Wasson, a wall street banker, attended one of her ceremonies. Wasson ended up writing a book about his experience -- what an idea, huh? -- and was featured on the cover of Life magazine. That brought an onslaught of psychedelic tourists to her Mazatec village in Mexico, including "Bob Dylan, John Lennon, and Keith Richards," among others.[8] These tourists had a negative effect on the village. It got bad enough that she was sent away and her house burned down. I believe it's important to remember and honor Maria Sabina. I also think it's an important lesson to carry forward during this third wave of psychedelics, to revere, respect, and preserve indigenous traditions and the natural resources from which we take the medicines.

If you decide to start your own personal journey into the rabbit hole, I would highly recommend getting to know the laws and the history around psychedelics.

Me and Drugs

As the son of a DEA agent, I had never tried a single drug, except alcohol, sugar, and caffeine -- all much more dangerous than psychedelics. But I'm getting

---

[8] https://en.wikipedia.org/wiki/Mar%C3%ADa_Sabina

ahead of myself. The point is, I thought psychedelics were bad drugs and that people who did them were bad people. The idea of me doing these was far from my normal thinking. But life wasn't normal anymore.

I read articles online. I joined communities, both online and in local groups. I learned all about the keys to a good psychedelic trip:

Set: Set is your mindset. Many people take this to mean that you're "ready" for a trip, but that isn't it. Mindset means you're prepared for the journey, which means you're ready to go into it and experience it, to let go, to open yourself to the lessons that you may learn.

Setting: Setting is the space in which you'll journey, including location, time of day, the setup of the space, and whether or not you'll have a sitter or guide or others with you. As for substance and dose, it's a matter of which psychedelic and how much of it. More details on how I chose those are in the appendices.

Substance and Dose: All psychedelics are unique. Some share similarities, like LSD and mushrooms. After all, LSD was created in pursuit of a synthetic mushroom. The mescaline cactuses, peyote and San Pedro, are similar. The point is, a journey will depend heavily on both the substance and the dosage ingested.

I'll spare you the play-by-play details of my journeys, unless I think the details are important to the story of my healing with my grief. But I will share the rough outline of a few important journeys with you now.

The First Trip: Mushrooms

I decided my first trip would be with psychedelic mushrooms: The Teachers. I chose to do a moderate dose of 2.8 grams. I had read, and have since confirmed, that doses in the 2.0-2.5 gram range can end up weird -- not hard, just strange. My setting was in a room, with a giant, comfy pillow to rest on. I had eye blinds and earplugs. I ran through my journey routine (appendices) which includes cleaning the house, covering clocks, showering, taking the dose, and meditating.

I was scared. Was I about to break my brain? I think that if I wasn't suffering grief, this fear would likely have kept me from doing this. But the deep pain I was feeling kind of gave me a feeling of, "How could it get worse?" Which might bring up the question of mindset again. Remember, it's not about being "happy". It's about being ready. And I was ready. Anxious and scared, yes, but ready.

I ate my mushrooms with great reverence. Yuck. They were terrible, a taste I've never gotten used to but now revere. I laid down onto the giant pillow, put on the blinds, and inserted the earplugs. And I waited. And waited.

Then I thought to myself, "These aren't working, they're not the right kind of mushrooms!"

Once I could tell the mushrooms were just fine and started feeling the "come up" of them working, I felt that nervousness -- "What have I done? Nevermind, I don't want to do this!" With a little reassurance and a focus on letting go, my nerves settled down and the trip began with some visuals.

I saw winding, white and red, snake-like fractal patterns growing, flowing, twisting in space. I heard the pulse in my ears beating, echoing. It sounded like something out of a Pink Floyd song. I started to laugh. Then I cried. Tears streamed down my cheeks. I thought, "This...THIS...is what they're talking about!" It's the same kind of reaction as to losing virginity, only times a thousand, and in the spiritual/mystical realm. It was awesome, heavy on the "awe."

It was absolutely magical, true to the mushrooms' adjective. Two images of my demons visited me, to tell me they've always been with me. But they let me know that while they are a part of me, they don't control me. I learned to appreciate my demons. I learned that what really matters is connections to the earth, nature, and other humans -- not things made of plastic, or glass, or metal. Those connections are a common experience with mushrooms and contribute to healing.

Healthy Body: Peyote

I'm lucky to live near legal Peyote. The Peyote Way Church is here in Arizona. After long, legal battles, they are able to grow and offer the sacred cactus to adherents. It is an amazing experience out there at the church in the desert. It's a three-day journey. The first day is for fasting, to make sure the body is ready for the sacrament. You arrive at the church, which is located on a 160-acre plot of desert land, on the afternoon prior to your Spirit Walk the following day. This first day is a time to wander the grounds, select your campsite, and contemplate.

The Church is a ranch house, with rooms for visitors to sleep, a gathering space with a wood stove (it's cold there), and a kitchen. The place is stocked with books on plant medicines and spirituality. Grab one and read!

The second day is the day of the Spirit Walk. The morning -- still fasting, no breakfast -- is crisp and available for more meditation and contemplation. I usually visit the Peyote greenhouses to spend time with these amazing cacti. Around 3pm, they gather us up, hand out the sacrament, and explain how to take it. Taking it is a six-hour process of sipping a tea that is disgusting, a tea that my body wants to reject from the very first sip. It is quite a challenge. But in my healing work, I've learned that lessons come during times of tension and torment. It's the same here.

Sacrament in hand, I headed out to my campsite with my gear -- sleeping bag, pillows, books, layers of clothes, and water. The water is for much later in the night, once I've consumed the tea.

I settled into my campsite, which is a canopy shading a spot with ground covered in carpeting, a lounge chair, a bucket of supplies (tissue, matches, flashlight, etc.), and a fire pit set up and ready to go.

Over the next several hours, I sipped Peyote tea and fought back nausea, eventually succumbing to the urge. At that point, the sun had set, replaced in the sky by a full moon. I was joined by owls, coyotes, and other desert creatures. The stars were bright and amazing. Once the temperature fell into misery territory, I gave the kindling a light and had a warm fire the rest of the night.

Peyote is very subtle (although the good folks at the Church don't agree with that description), unlike the punch-in-the-face teachings of the mushrooms. During the night, I had a mental clarity that typically only comes with those special moments in meditation. It was as if my left brain was turned off. It almost felt as if not much was happening at all, but I know something was going on, as I remained wide awake all night.

Eventually, the moon set, and the sun popped up over the distant mountain range on the horizon. My journey was over. I put out the fire, poured water on it, and reset my campsite back to how I had found it. I gathered my gear up and trekked in the freezing cold back to the church.

After loading my gear into my car, I went into the church. The other adherents had already returned (they came back in the middle of the night, which is not uncommon) and were sleeping. A slow cooker full of beans waited for me. I scooped out a serving, dropped in some hot sauce, and warmed my belly. I sat in the common area, waiting for the minister to show up with my car keys. After getting my keys and a deep hug, I got in my car and made the three-hour trip home.

So, what happened? It was hard to tell. The whole three-day trip is something unlike anything I had ever experienced. It took me about a week to process it. At the end of that week, I could no longer eat meat.

Going vegetarian was really weird for me. I was a true carnivore -- I hated (and still do) vegetables. I once ate a hot dog stuffed in a hamburger wrapped in bacon. I used to eat 32oz steaks. So I was confused by this. As of writing this, almost four years later, I'm still a vegetarian.

I think the Peyote saved my life. At least, it added years to the end of my life. My diet was killing me. My guts were falling apart, sometimes literally bleeding to tell me something was wrong. After dropping meat, adding some fiber, and counting my calories, I dropped over sixty pounds, and I felt much better.

I've been back to the Church twice more since that first journey. Each time, the sacrament opens up my pure consciousness and quiets my monkey brain. Under the moon and stars, out there in the Arizona desert, a Peyote journey is very deep and special.

Healthy Mind: Ayahuasca

I did intense, psychoanalytical, Freudian talk therapy for years, and it was huge in helping me get things straight in life. Roughly four years and $40,000 of it with an amazing therapist, and I was able to gain insight into my psyche, things like why I bristled at people trying to help me, why I hated myself, why my temper was always locked and loaded. I am still grateful for that work. But one weekend with La Madre, the spirit of Ayahuasca, did for me what maybe two to three years of therapy did.

This particular Ayahuasca journey was roughly my third or fourth weekend with the medicine, over a four year period. My other experiences were relatively uneventful, and I was starting to think that Ayahuasca just wasn't what it was cut out to be. Or that it just didn't work for me. At a previous ceremony, I had even complained to the facilitator about these "light" experiences, especially as compared to my mushrooms. On the second night, he gave me a huge dose. Nothing. I purged four times, so he saw my night as successful. But I got nothing out of it.

But this time was different. The ceremony started just like all the others. It was a small group of maybe six participants and three facilitators. They took us through the typical rituals of cleaning the air and our bodies with burning sage, passed around ceremonial tobacco, and had each of us share our intentions. Then, one by one, we approached the altar and received our dose of the medicina -- Ayahuasca.

This particular facilitator trains in South America each year to learn from the Shipibo shamans there and to brew a batch of Ayahuasca. She does a single brew for both the initial and follow-on doses. Some facilitators will brew two different concoctions for each stage of the journey.

I received my dose, returned to my spot in the room, and waited. I had my typical experience, up to a point. The visuals were strong. Time evaporated into the cosmic ether. My consciousness grew, while my monkey-mind quieted down. I waited to purge, which didn't happen right away. Purging is typically barfing, but it can take the form of laughing, crying, pooping, orgasming, and more. I always throw up, as I heard others doing already. One woman couldn't stop laughing. No purge yet for me.

I went outside once I started to feel myself return to Earth. I wanted to be with the stars and the clean, crisp air. As I sat outside, my mind entered a really special, contemplative state. It's a state of mind like that described by St. John of the Cross in *Dark Night of the Soul,* where a ray of divine light illuminated my soul, allowing me to receive a new message should I choose to put them in the light. That's a bit woo-woo, but that's the headspace I was in. It was beautiful, and I wanted it to continue.

I went back inside to sit at the altar and get another dose, a booster dose. I wanted this mindset to continue and hoped a booster dose could accomplish that.

There was another participant at the altar, getting help. In the fetal position, he obviously needed some attention. I finally decided it was going to be a while, so I went back to my spot, leaned up against the wall, and closed my eyes. I decided I didn't need a second dose, that I'd just ride this out and get some rest. While I didn't have any breakthrough, once again, it was at least heady, and I was ready to retire.

That's when things got real. The visuals came back just as strong as if I'd just take the first dose. The visuals were amazing. I focused on them. And then they kind of froze, almost looking back at me. I realized then that these visuals were La Madre, the Ayahuasca spirit. She connected with me, conveyed to me, "You don't need a second dose to see me. I'm always here. I am you." Right then, she built -- manifested -- this shiny metallic cylinder. It had these medieval metal spikes on it, like the thorns of a rose. She wrapped the cylinder in what I call mind ribbon -- a black hole-like ribbon where time and light disappeared. Then she held it out to me and conveyed, "Get rid of this." And I purged. I threw up right into my barf bucket. But more importantly, I purged that dark object that La Madre had created for me. What was this thing I purged?

It was a sense of feeling powerless to make change in my life. Even after all that therapy and other growth in life, I carried around this notion that shit just happened to me -- my parent's divorce, my son dying by suicide. I had this feeling that no matter what I did, things would fall apart, and that I didn't have the power to make any changes. La Madre helped me purge that notion and opened a door to a new way of thinking.

Oneness: The Toad

I debated with myself as to whether I should include this section in the book. "The Toad" is the incilius alvarius, or Desert Sonoran Toad (a.k.a. Bufo alvarius or just "bufo"). This animal is an amazing inhabitant of the Sonoran Desert, where I live. It basically sleeps through most of the year, until the monsoons come. They then emerge from the burrows they stole from other animals and begin eating and mating. But the magic is in the poison they create.

The toad's poison contains a chemical called 5-Meo-DMT, one of the two main DMT drugs you may have heard about. DMT, when smoked, goes straight to the brain and creates a short (15-20 minute) journey that is unlike other psychedelic journeys.

In my Toad session, I had a facilitator -- a beautiful soul -- who walked me through the process. It was a matter of inhaling the vaporized poison in the form of smoke, which I did. I inhaled the smoke and immediately laid back onto a comfortable bed with plush pillows. Before my head hit the pillows, I was no longer in this time and space.

A giant portal broke open in space, and I flowed through it. I saw (not with my eyes) every being that ever existed in time, bound together by threads of white energy. It wasn't a visual experience. It was of an essence. It was essential in a different meaning of that word.

Psychonauts -- those who regularly partake in psychedelics -- like to talk about "ego death", a term coined by Timothy Leary. They really like to talk about it. The irony is that "ego death" becomes an ego trip in the community. It is an experience where you feel like you kind of died, that your "I" is gone, no more self. That's what happened to me during this experience. My soul had left my body and was out in the universal consciousness that may be what the after-life is all about. I don't know. But I was out there and didn't want to return to my gross, lizard-body. "Yuck!" I thought, as I felt my own skin-covered body. It was crazy.

The lesson I took from this is two-fold. One, I experienced a new reality. Yes, that happens with just about every psychedelic trip, but with this one, reality shifted for sure. And two, I experienced that "One-ness" of it all in a very real sense. That feeling would become an essential part of my grief trip.

What Psychedelics Taught Me

My psychedelic experience was very analogous to St. John of the Cross's dark night of the soul, but I might go all hippie and call it the "high-vibe morning of the soul." Psychedelics taught me what I needed to learn, and I think that's no coincidence. Deep in my psyche, in my unconscious -- what psychonauts and Carl Jung call "The Shadow" -- are those things that affect my life. They can bubble up into waking consciousness at any moment and wreak havoc. And that's where grief can hide -- in the unconscious mind -- until one of those landmines lets it out.

Psychedelics, much like other non-ordinary states of consciousness like dreams, open up that unconscious space for examination. But here's the thing. Very rarely were those hidden pieces of my psyche ever directly related to grief. In order to heal with my grief, I need to heal, period. I needed to heal other pain, trauma, and negative thoughts and emotions. I needed to heal my body along with my mind. As you saw in my stories above, psychedelics helped me do just that.

When I heal, I can then love myself. When I can love myself, I can have compassion for my state of grief. It's like there's this angry, broken child in my heart. I can't heal him by punishing him, by yelling at him, or by abandoning him. I have to love him, and I can only give him love once I learn to love myself and to forgive myself. Let me tell you, I'm not there, yet. While I have made tremendous progress, there is always more work to do.

There is always what my teacher calls "the next message" waiting for me. Psychedelics open the door to that next message.

That's what psychedelics taught me. They taught me to love myself, to be true to myself, to accept myself. When I do those things, then I can embrace my grief with love and learn to heal with my grief. I'm not always successful in staying true to myself. Some might say rarely, even. But those moments are important.

My Grief Trip

When I tell this story of loss, grief, and psychedelics, I get all kinds of reactions, but one question that is common. "Okay, so now you're a hippie. But is it helping with your grief?" Great question. And the answer is complex and involves my grief trip.

Fair warning, there's going to be some Eastern philosophy/religion here. But with that warning, I'll repeat what a teacher of mine pointed out. Philosophies, religions, teachings, beliefs...they're all maps of what I believe is the same path, the same way, to happiness, or at least contentment.

Happiness? Can I find happiness in this deep well of sadness? Yes. I have an analogy for these two seemingly mutually exclusive emotions -- happiness and sadness. The analogy is brain waves. You've heard of an EEG (electroencephalograph). It measures brain activity, brain waves. There are a handful of brain waves, depending on your state of concentration or consciousness: Delta:sleep, Theta:daydreaming, Alpha:alert readiness; Beta: concentration, etc. I say we have brain waves for sadness and happiness. They're both always there, but one may be stronger or more active at any given moment. We raise the vibrations of those waves on demand. Or, like a guitar string, they can be plucked into high vibrations by an external force.

My mother once asked me if I can be happy. I took a moment to dig around in my box of feelings and right there under the pile of grief was a bit of happiness. "Yes, I can be happy. I am happy." And I know I can be sad at any given moment by just stepping on one of those landmines. The two emotions -- brain waves -- are always present in me and in everyone, I believe.

Psychedelics have opened my mind and my heart and allowed me to work on myself, something I've had to do -- save myself first, put the airplane's air mask on myself first. But that has been tough. You see, part of my psyche has been self-loathing and self-denial. If you ever tried to offer me something nice in the past, I would have declined it, feeling unworthy. I was stuck. I needed to learn how to move forward.

Open The Gates

Ram Dass has this concept called, "The Next Message." There is always a next message waiting for me, and it's always right where I am, right when I am. I just have to be ready to accept it. Psychedelics have a way of bringing me to that next message. In fact, on one journey, the mushrooms showed me the entire path in an amazing visual space. It was like Dorothy's yellow brick road but in fractal, strong-pastel bricks. Along the road, I passed through portals -- next messages. I eventually landed right back where I started, after weaving my way through different planes of time and reality. But it's important to note that I ended up back here, now.

You see, this journey, this grief trip, is one of finding my path. It's not about finding myself. It's not about healing. It's not about coming to terms with my grief, with my loss. It's about finding the way, the path in life. I like to say that when I'm centered, caught in that space of equilibrium, going with life's river (flow), I am able to have strength. I'm able to have compassion, generosity, humility. I feel centered. And that helps me live with my grief.

In the end, psychedelics are not a cure for grief. They helped me find peace, understanding, and connection to other people, to my soulmate, my beautiful daughter, other people, and to nature. When I have that sense of peace, a lack of contention, no longer always controlled by craving for attachments, then I'm able to truly be in the moment. In that space, grief is real. It just is. And it's right here with me, at this moment. That means I live with it, I heal with it. It's not something from my past that haunts me. It's not something in my future that I crave or need to lose or to be free from. That feeling is very freeing. And psychedelics showed me the way.

On this grief trip, there are three components, much like in yoga, that I have experienced as being important to my being able to heal with my grief. They are body, mind, and spirit -- and note on reincarnation. Spirit is a funny one, given my deep, rational skepticism. But a few trips down that rabbit hole will get you thinking.

Body

Those landmines, the way they can set my whole self -- mind, body, and spirit -- into a grief spiral, are worthy of notice and some self-defense. One of the best ways to set up a defense against them is to prepare my body. Now, don't get me wrong. I'm not some lean vegan destined to live into my 100s. I still have a habit of overeating on weekends, including way too much sugar. But those bad habits also give me a control, a baseline to make observations and comparisons.

When I eat right, a good balance in my calories of protein, carbohydrates, fat, and fiber, my body is ready to defend against the explosions. My nerves are settled. My brain has the right amount of oxygen and glucose, and my blood carries the right nutrients. There is a sense of calmness and control.

I feel like nutrition and exercise are two sides, yin and yang, of the same coin. Getting my heart pumping two to three times a week during my morning jogs has been tremendously helpful.

My goal, physically, is to find that nice, quiet equilibrium space in my body. When my body is centered, my mind is more easily centered, and I am better prepared to continue to grow, react, and just be.

Curious as to how I lost the weight? Check my weight-loss regimen in the Appendices.

Mind

When Ian died, I became curious about human consciousness. I wanted to know if it survives death. Is there a kind of a soul that goes on after the body has died? What does consciousness even mean? So many questions. I attempted to answer them in my podcast, The Consciousness Podcast. Some things I discovered in those interviews and in my psychedelic journeys were very helpful.

As one goes out into the "spiritual" world of woo-woo, you'll discover talk of "planes of consciousness." At first, I resisted these notions, my rational brain not allowing me to accept too much of that stuff. But I've come to see consciousness in three levels: sensual (body), mind (ego), and pure consciousness (awareness).

Many psychedelic explorers spend time trying to kill their egos. Remember when I talked about ego death, that's what it's called. It's like this weird egoic badge of psychonautic honor. Like I said earlier, I see it as a total ego trip. And I spent years trying to kill, or transcend, my own ego. Heck, my chosen teacher, the late Ram Dass, regularly taught that one needs to transcend the ego in order to find higher consciousness and break from desires and, by extension, grief. It turns out that the ego is a beautiful thing. Without it, we'd likely not survive. It solves problems, helps us be creative, seeks out pleasure. But it also won't shut up. In fact, it can feel at times, at least it did to me, that my ego thrives in turmoil like grief. Feelings and emotions like grief provide a framework of drama around which my mind can rally and start taking over. That can end up being a dark place.

Psychedelics help find that calm place. In fact, there are ideas in the neuroscience world that your ego is the part of your brain called the default mode network (DMN), which integrates different areas of your brain. Some studies seem to show that psychedelics quiet down the DMN. Maybe they are shutting up that beautiful ego? But we're not seeking a lobotomy here. We just want some control, some quiet. And psychedelics show us that's possible. They even give us a taste of a method to get that quiet -- meditation.

They key to the mind on our grief trip is understanding that it's a functioning organ in our bodies, just like the pancreas. It's job is to spit out thoughts, ideas, and memories. That's what it's going to do. Psychedelics can help get in touch with that, understand it, accept it, and work with it.

I also think there are two levels of thoughts: mindful thoughts and those excretion thoughts. Excretion thoughts are that monkey mind, just random memories, fantasies, predictions, reminders, etc. and the emotions tied to them. It's my mind doing its best to keep me alive. Mindful thoughts are those moments when I'm concentrating without the interruptions of those other excretion thoughts. That's a great space to be in. It's in that space where I can really dig into my grief and my love without losing it.

Spirit

The idea of me talking about "Spirit" or spirituality is kind of funny, given my lifelong belief in nothing but science. God? Nope. Spirit? Nope. Ghosts? Reincarnation? Little green men? Crystals? 432Hz? None of it. That said, having been through these journeys, it is quite hard for me to deny that there might be more to all this. I definitely feel a connection to all living beings. I see humans as souls now, possibly all individual points of a greater consciousness collapsed into a single point, known as Stuart, or Sara, or Louise, or Ian.

As I meditate and continue new journeys and read from books, my connection to the spiritual side of my awareness grows stronger. As it does, my intuitive understanding of grief and souls also grows.

The point, when it comes to spirit and grief, is that accepting that cosmic, universal connection -- that

Oneness -- helps to quiet my mind and find compassion for others. When I do that, it gives my mind and my awareness the space to grieve without it becoming debilitating.

A Note On Reincarnation

I include this part on reincarnation because most of us have lost somebody close to us. You come into this grief trip with your own set of beliefs, maybe even with a religious background. I come into it, as I mentioned, with full on skepticism. However, I read an interesting book by Dr. Jim Tucker (University of Virginia's Department of Psychiatry and Neurobehavioral Sciences[9]) called *Life Before LIfe*, in which Dr. Tucker lays out a pretty compelling case for reincarnation based on substantial circumstantial evidence. The most famous example is a young boy who remembers dying in World War II, as a pilot flying from an aircraft carrier off of Japan. The kid remembered details that aren't public. It's a little freaky. It really made me think: if this is true, then what else might be true? What is my faith in rational science keeping me from understanding?

I'm not saying that I buy into the karma part of reincarnation -- neither does Dr. Tucker, by the way -- but the whole concept is hard to find fault with . If you combine that with his colleague's study of Near Death

---

9

https://med.virginia.edu/perceptual-studies/dops-staff/jim-tuckers-bio/

eriences (Dr. Bruce Greyson[10]), there seems to be something there. And then here come psychedelics.

Psychedelic journeys bring you into new realities, much like dreams. You see things and experience levels of consciousness and reality that you never thought possible. Maybe, like me, you even denied them. Oftentimes, these realms provide messages similar to those messages received by NDE experiencers -- that there's something greater out there, to love each other, a great connection to nature, a feeling of Oneness. Doesn't that notion have a significant effect on your grief or at least for the possibilities with your grief?

10

https://med.virginia.edu/perceptual-studies/our-research/near-death-experiences-ndes/

Epilogue:
Continued Healing

Here I am, five years after losing Ian. Writing that sentence wells up sorrow in my heart. Grief and sadness are still very much here with me. But when I think over these five years and the healing I've done, I am so completely grateful for psychedelics. I don't know how I could have made it without the help from these amazing medicines. That said, I'm going to surprise you. I'm not here to tell you to use drugs. I'm not saying anybody **should** use psychedelics. As I mentioned above, there are many paths on which to take your grief trip. It may seem like psychedelics were my path, but the truth is they just turned on the street lights so that I could see my path.

Ironically, even after many psychedelic journeys, I still don't understand The Grateful Dead. But Jerry Garcia has a great quote:

> "Life is my yoga, too, but I've been a spiritual dilettante off and on through the years, trying various things at various times, and I firmly believe that every avenue that leads to higher consciousness does lead to higher consciousness. If you think it does, it does. If you put energy into it on a daily basis, no matter what it is, some discipline, or whatever it is, I believe it will work. I believe that it's within the power of the mind and consciousness to do that."

Every avenue leads to higher consciousness, he points out. Getting to that higher consciousness on your grief trip, in my opinion, is a key to surviving, to moving forward, to healing with your grief. It was for me. That also means that psychedelics don't have to be the light that illuminates your path. I believe, when you look, you'll find your way.

Healing with Grief

Throughout this writing, I've been talking about "healing with my grief." I think the "with" is an important distinction. I didn't do this on purpose. Maybe some smart person like my wife or a friend or therapist told me not to try and heal FROM my grief, but I don't remember it. Throughout my journeys, I emerged with two concurrent feelings: happiness and sadness. Contentment and grief, at the same time. In looking at that, I realized that I wasn't trying to put grief away. I wasn't trying to move on. Moving on. That concept feels too insulting, to my experience, to my love for my son, and to my deep respect for him. There is no moving on. But I can exist with my grief; with my memories of him. That is learning to heal WITH grief, and that is what my grief trip was really all about.

Breaking Stigmas

I've been very open about my grief, about the way Ian died, and about my use of psychedelics. I've gone too far with my openness, sometimes being insensitive to the impact hearing Ian's story can have on others. I once looked up into the mirror at my hair dresser's place to see her crying after I nonchalantly answered her question, "Yes, I have two kids: a 17-year-old daughter and a son who died at 19 by suicide." Careless of me.

My openness about these subjects has led people to tell me that I'm brave for doing so. Frankly, I don't feel brave. I feel broken and sad, and often lost and confused. But the more they told me that, the more I felt like maybe there was something here. Like the old song by Buffalo Springfield, maybe "Something's happening here."

That "something" is the breaking of stigmas. When I talk about mental health, suicide, and psychedelics, then I'm helping to make it normal to talk about these things. My hope is that you'll also talk about them. The more we talk and share, the more we break the stigmas around these issues. When we break those stigmas, people are more likely to seek help. When they seek help, maybe they won't die.

Thank you for reading this far. My heart is with you.

Appendix: The Psychedelics

Safety First

Many of these are probably illegal where you live. Don't take chances. Don't break the law. If you can find a legal setting, then consider the following in order to reduce the risk of harm to yourself:

1. Have a trip sitter. Have a sober person in the same space or dwelling who can come to your aid if needed.
2. Test your substances. Get test kits and test your drugs. A friend of a friend lost his life thinking he was using LSD. It was laced. He's dead. Test your drugs[11].
3. Don't mix with other medicines. If you're taking any kind of drugs, talk to your doctor. Best case is that you just don't trip. Worst case is you die. Don't mix.
4. Create a safe container. If you're with friends or in a ceremony, make it safe. Have a first aid kit. Have an evacuation plan. Set rules for things like consent.
5. Know your mental health history. If you or your family has any history of psychosis, such as bipolar disorder or schizophrenia, do not take these drugs. Consult your doctor.

The Psychedelics

---

[11] https://dancesafe.org/

Magic Mushrooms: The most common psychoactive mushrooms are the psilocybe cubensis. There are probably tens of varieties of these with names like B+ (Be Positive), Penis Envy, and Golden Teachers. You'll hear different stories about potency, but they're pretty much all the same. The doses tend to range this way:

- 1g-1.5g: This is a light dose, or "sparkly" as a friend calls it. I have had some very deep experiences at 1.5g.
- 1.5g-2.5g: Avoid this range, and it can leave you in this weird, in-between space and just feels weird.
- 2.8-4.2g: This is a deep trip. You'll still know your zip code, but the mushrooms are going to bring you some deep lessons.
- 5g and beyond: This is the proverbial "heroic" dose made famous by Terrance McKenna. You may not know what a zip code is. You may not even exist any longer. Be careful here.

I recommend starting at around 2.8g for your first experience.

Ayahuasca: Don't do Ayahuasca alone. Do it in a ceremony. Go to Peru or Central America, and find a trusted center. There's also one in Orlando called Soul Quest. A good facilitator[12] will control the dose and the

---

[12]

https://doorofperception.com/wp-content/uploads/Ayahuasca-Manifesto_Anonymous_May-1st-2012.pdf setting. It's a magical experience with song (Icaros), ceremony, and other souls. You'll start with one drink of Ayahuasca, typically about the size of a shot glass. You'll be offered additional doses as the night goes on. Take them when called to do so. Don't force it.

LSD: LSD typically comes in "tabs" of paper, about a square centimeter, or in gels. It's hard to know what the dose actually is. It's likely between 100 and 200 micrograms (mics). A dose is considered 100 micrograms. I suggest starting with a ½ to a ¾ of a dose your first time.

Peyote: Peyote will also be experienced in a ceremonial setting. Just like with Ayahuasca, go with a trusted group. I love The Peyote Way Church in Arizona. Great people. Peyote is either a tea you drink or cactus "buttons" you chew. Either way, it's totally gross. San Pedro, another psychoactive cactus containing mescaline, is pretty much the same as Peyote.

Other Psychedelics: DMT, 5-Meo-DMT, MDMA, and scores of synthetic substances are out there. I told my story of 5-Meo-DMT, and it was powerful for me. However, in the context of your work with grief, these substances are not necessary. Come to them when called, if called. If not, feel confident to leave them alone.

Appendix: Journey Checklist

When it comes to (mind)set and setting, this is a sample checklist to help prepare both mind and space.

1. Fast (no eating) for 6 hours before ingesting.
2. Clean up the space: no dust, no stains, etc. You'll really see those when your awareness is heightened.
3. Have your playlist ready. That means download it. You don't want it live-streamed, as that'll mean your phone is connected to the real world, and you don't want that. Music is optional[13].
4. NO caffeine, chocolate, coffee, tea beforehand or during.
5. Read from your holy book, if applicable.
6. Meditate: clear your mind. Allow anxiety-driven thoughts to come, and go.
7. Prepare the medicine for ingestion.
8. Put your phone on airplane mode.
9. Get a pad, pencil/pen ready. Don't write down every little thing, or you'll lose your space. Write down the insights, the epiphanies.
10. Hide clocks. Knowing the time brings you back to earth.

---

[13] I believe in a dark, quiet setting with no music, especially during the come-up and peaks. Once you enter the come-down, music is okay. But music, in my opinion, has too large of an impact on the journey, so I recommend leaving your mindspace free to explore what it needs.

11. Have comfort ready to go: blankets, pillows, clothes, etc.

12. Write out the reason you're doing this: your intention. And then let it go,

13. If you're worried you'll freak out, put stickies around that say, "Relax, you're on drugs."

14. Ingest: Take your medicine.

15. You have about 30 minutes. Poop, shower, dress, and get comfortable.

16. Say to yourself, "I don't know. I don't know where I will go now. I don't know." That releases expectations.

17. Optional: slide on your eye covers and put in the earplugs.

18. And you're off….

Appendix: Psychedelic Internet Resources

https://maps.org/ This is the first place I send everybody. Their mission: "Founded in 1986, the Multidisciplinary Association for Psychedelic Studies (MAPS) is a 501(c)(3) non-profit research and educational organization that develops medical, legal, and cultural contexts for people to benefit from the careful uses of psychedelics and marijuana."

MAPS Psychedelic Integration List A list of people who can help you integrate your lessons or experiences.

Erowid Great overall source of information on psychedelics. "Erowid is a member-supported organization providing access to reliable, non-judgmental information about psychoactive plants, chemicals, and related issues."

Zendo Project This group is THE resource for harm reduction. Spend some time on this site.

DanceSafe.org Always...ALWAYS...test your substances. This organization is doing great things keeping people safe at festivals, raves, etc. Use their test kits.

KetamineHelps.com This is my wife's site. It's a great resource for information on Ketamine.

Psychedelic Seminars This group does live and archived video discussions on all topics related to Psychedelics.

ThirdWave "Resources for safe, structured, and responsible psychedelic use."

Psychedelic Today This is pretty much THE podcast on psychedelics. I've had both Kyle and Joe on my podcasts.

Trip Safe This site has some really good info on what trips are like, the dangers of each psychedelic, etc. Whatever you're considering trying, check here for info.

Appendix: Weight-Loss Program

Three times in my adult life, I've lost 40+ pounds. After the second time, I declared that'd be the last time, that if I gained it all back again, I'd just have to die early like my dad did. Then, I lost Ian, and things changed. I want to live for my daughter. I want to live for myself, too, and for my wife. But I want my daughter to have her dad around for a full life. So, I decided to do this a third time.

This time, I have kept my weight off for over a year. In fact, I'm still 20 pounds lighter than when I ran my first (and last) marathon. And I thought that was going to be a good weight for the rest of my life. I never imagined I'd get back to my old military weight and keep it there.

Anyway, here's what I did and my recommendations:

1.   Take your "before" photo now. You'll thank me.
2.   Install My Fitness Pal on your phone.
3.   Use My Fitness Pal to calculate your daily calorie intake and log everything you eat. I think this habit is the most important aspect of this whole plan.
4.   Stop eating junk food, fast food, soda, and alcohol. Forever. Sure, you can have these anytime you want but no longer as a habit. I'd recommend dropping or greatly reducing meat as well (beef, pork, and chicken at the very least).

5.   Water and Fiber. Drink lots of water and make sure you get your fiber. You likely need about 20-30g of fiber per day.

6.   Start your day with a smoothie. I'm not talking about a dessert smoothie like you get at Jamba Juice, full of sugar. You want a serving of fruit, a serving of leafy greens, some protein, water, fiber, and omega fats. See my recipe at the end of this appendix.

7.   Add three days of aerobic exercise. No pain. You just want your heart beating for a good 45 minutes, three times a week. Consult your doctor before starting, though.

8.   Get a blood test (and then again every year). You want to know if you're eating the right nutrients: sugar, fat, iron, Vitamin D, B12, etc.

9.   Weigh yourself once a week, on the same day, after your exercise that day, fully nude. Don't weigh yourself outside of that weigh-in.

10.   Note on calorie counting: I stick to the calorie totals pretty strictly, but I also give myself a free day to eat pretty much whatever I want. I believe, based on experience and what I read in some other, low-carb diet books, that you can fool your body into not using all those calories if you only overdo it once a week. Just don't let this throw you off for the rest of the week. That really means don't eat or drink trigger foods that have after-effects. That would likely include a ton of

sugar or alcohol. Those make you want more, for at least a day after you consume them.

My Smoothie Recipe

.5-1 cup frozen fruit

.5-1 cup frozen greens (kale, spinach)

.5-1 cup organic, greek, whole milk yogurt

Scoop of organic pea protein

Scoop of Super Green food powder

Scoop of ground flax seeds (fiber and omegas)

2 Tablespoons of hemp hearts (omegas)

1 Tablespoon apple cider vinegar

1 Tablespoon honey

Daily Meal Plan

Breakfast: Smoothie and 3 brazil nuts

Morning Snack: Banana

Lunch: Half of an Amy's cheese pizza; or Veggie Burger and an apple; or Grilled cheese sandwiches; or Tostadas (2)

Afternoon Snack: Apple and mixed nuts

Dinner: Frozen burrito or something around 200-300 calories

Dessert: Dark chocolate (100 calorie portion); it can have caramel & sea salt or nuts, etc.